The Race

without

Rivalry

The Race

without

Rivalry

PETER BAIBAI

The Race without Rivalry

iUniverse books may be ordered through booksellers or by contacting:

iUniverse
1663 Liberty Drive
Bloomington, IN 47403
www.iuniverse.com
1-800-Authors (1-800-288-4677)

Because of the dynamic nature of the Internet, any web addresses or links contained in this book may have changed since publication and may no longer be valid. The views expressed in this work are solely those of the author and do not necessarily reflect the views of the publisher, and the publisher hereby disclaims any responsibility for them.

Any people depicted in stock imagery provided by Thinkstock are models, and such images are being used for illustrative purposes only. Certain stock imagery © Thinkstock.

Scripture quotations marked KJV are from the Holy Bible, King James Version (Authorized Version). First published in 1611. Quoted from the KJV Classic Reference Bible, Copyright © 1983 by The Zondervan Corporation.

ISBN: 978-1-4917-6735-1 (sc)
ISBN: 978-1-4917-6736-8 (e)

Library of Congress Control Number: 2015906827

Print information available on the last page.

iUniverse rev. date: 06/12/2015

To you my wonderful children—Jonathan, Eliezer; Sabbath, Destinie; Baibai Jr., and Elisabeth

May you run your race and enjoy to the fullest the privilege our Lord has bestowed upon you.

Acknowledgments

All though we are many and differ in callings in life, we are one in one sense, the people of one God who saved us by sending His son who came down to this world to redeem us from sin. I am so grateful for the wisdom, knowledge, and inspiration you all gave to me—whether mentally, socially, and spiritually—enabling me to come this far one way or other. I feel a deep sense of appreciation and gratitude to:

- All my teachers, friends, colleagues, and employers who have taught and imparted knowledge to me, challenged me, and refined me to be able to accomplish my purpose.
- All my fellow Christians and churches of believers of Christ Jesus in Papua New Guinea and abroad for all your encouragement and blessings through your words, letters, emails, and books. Our God is so good.

And in relation to this book, I give my sincere thanks and gratitude to:

- The very special people in my life who continually (and occasionally) give advice and encouragement to me after reading some of my poems to writing this book, namely Elijah Malaur, Regina Kawai, Alfred Murliu, Anton Boboko, and Michael Daula of Rabaul; Francis Leba, Aloise Rangan, and Advent Fidelis of OISCA International; and Jonathan Danny and

Hapon Hapakali of Ok Tedi Mining Ltd, all of Papua New Guinea.

- My immediate brothers and sisters—Sr. Marie Norbert Baibai, Paskalis Iringa, Joseph, and Mathias Baibai—for the love and support you gave concerning this book. What you have done made me come to know God in such a deeper way, enabling me to write about this love and grace that He has given us only through His love, His son, our Lord Jesus Christ. Thank you, and I love you all.

- My beloved, modest wife Alice and children—Jonathan, Eliezer; Sabbath, Destinie; Baibai Jr., and Elisabeth—for your unwavering and earnest support, help, love, and inspiration that you have given me to the development of this book and your belief that the truth, life, and love of God can also be spread through writing, even poetry.

Contents

Introduction

*Wherefore seeing we also are compassed about with
so great a cloud of witnesses, let us lay aside every weight,
and the sin which doth so easily beset us, and let us run with
patience the race that is set before us* (Heb. 12:1, KJV).

*For every one that asketh receiveth; and he that seeketh findeth;
and to him that knocketh it shall be opened* (Matt. 7:8, KJV).

*If ye then, being evil, know how to give good gifts
unto your children, how much more shall your Father
which is in heaven give good things to them
that ask him?* (Matt. 7:11, KJV).

Have you ever asked the Lord why He created Satan, the devil, and Lucifer? And did you ever think of asking the Lord for what purpose He created and made everything seen and unseen, darkness and light, good and evil? It can take quite a while to come up with answers to these questions, depending on how sincere and earnest one is in finding them.

Lo, we can never fully have that privilege in Christ if we don't have the knowledge from above. We can never ever receive anything if we keep restraining ourselves from asking Him. Or we can never ever be successful if we keep on running like fools. And we can never find any treasure if we have not been diving. Swimmers collect debris and floating objects, and wreckage remains. But divers find riches and treasures of the deep.

How This Book Got Its Title

The Race without Rivalry came about due to a true series of events that took place from June 1–21, 2001(in the poem, *The Journey Part 1-4*). This man named Villa asked the Lord an unusual and daring—but life-changing—question concerning Satan and the devil. As a conventional Christian, Villa had been living and thinking that the root cause of his everyday problems and troubles he faced in life were often caused by evil beings and this person called Satan or the devil. He thought that, if he only knew the evil one's strategies, ways, and tactics, he could easily counter them and be a victor over him every day. But one day, he came face-to-face with the One who created Satan and evil and found something he had never expected, known, and heard of before from any person—men or medium—in all his lifetime.

And that night, as he sat down to say his last prayer of the greatest event of his life, he said, "Show me Satan, o Lord, and his ways, and that shall be sufficient for me."

The Lord just smiled at him and said, "How can it be possible for you to know this created being and his ways if you don't even know who created him? In other words, how can you know Satan if you don't even know me, his Creator? Behold! You will never ever know him if you are thinking of bypassing the knowledge about me, for I am the truth of who evil really is. I know your thoughts and strength. They are all out against this creation of mine, which you and other men have not truly come to know his mission and purpose on earth. If only you know what I want you to know, you will live in total peace, as if Satan doesn't exist."

For as the heavens are higher than the earth, so
my ways higher than your ways, and my thoughts
than your thoughts (Isa. 55:09, KJV).

But seek ye first the kingdom of God, and his righteousness;
and all these things shall be added unto you (Matt. 6:33, KJV).

I form the light, and create darkness: I make peace,
and create evil: I the LORD do all these things (Isa. 45:7, KJV).

What? shall we receive good at the hand of God,
and shall we not receive evil? (Job 2:10, KJV).

Villa could not say anything. He just sat there numbed, staring at nothing and not saying anything until he dropped onto his bed that was made from the brush of the wild. And he was woken up late the next day by beasts of the wilderness, which much is to be said of. From then on, his life was never again the same. The revelation and understanding that God is the author of good and evil has given him rest from the fear and anxiety of the evil one all these years. You will find out just a little bit more about this person called Villa as you read on and get to the end of this book.

The Aim of This Book

As you have seen, this book is written in poetry format and purposely written to inspire and instigate every believer of Christ Jesus to seek God further, going beyond his or her present level of understanding of God and acquiring his ever-unlimited riches, which are still not known to men.

As we are witnessing all around us, year after year, mankind is always progressing, tapping into new and very sophisticated and complex technology that has never been seen before. And sometimes it is very difficult to understand these innovations and contrivances. In the spirit, there is much more than these which God is willing to reveal to us, things we've never ever seen or heard of before. Yet we seem to limit ourselves, depending on others and living with the same revelations or *manna* of yesterday, thinking that is all the Lord could offer. Let me tell you that God is unlimited and has much more than you can ever imagine or think of because the knowledge of God is like a never-ending horizon.

Therefore, if you are fed up of the daily deadly religious games or have been spoon-fed all these times by others, it is time you become a grown-up and a mature being, having to gather your own food, cook your own meal, and eat by yourself instead of someone else always holding the spoon for you. It is time to let go of the mortal and boldly draw near to the throne of grace, seeking God as never before. It does not matter whether you are a doctor, pastor, leader, or ordinary person or what color of skin you have. God sees into the heart and not the mantle. He is color-blind. When He looks at you, He does not see a black or white man. He sees only the righteousness of His son, if you dare believe that. God is wisdom himself, and He is full of knowledge and understanding. And He will gladly welcome anyone anywhere who genuinely and sincerely seeks Him with his or her heart to know the truth and depths of heaven, even the revelation of Jesus Christ.

But as it is written, Eye hath not seen, nor ear heard,
neither have entered into the heart of man, the things which
God hath prepared for them that love him (1 Cor. 2:9, KJV).

For this is the covenant that I will make with the house of Israel
after those days, saith the Lord; I will put my laws into their mind,
and write them in their hearts: and I will be to them a God,
and they shall be to me a people: And they shall not teach every
man his neighbour, and every man his brother, saying,
Know the Lord: for all shall know me, from the
least to the greatest (Heb. 8:10, KJV).

You see! God wants everyone to seek Him personally so He may put His laws in our minds and write them in our hearts, for we are the spiritual Israel. And when that is done, no one will be able to teach another person, his neighbor, and even his brother or sister about whom God really is, for every one of us shall know our God by heart and mind, from the very least person to the greatest, whoever cares to believe this good news.

As you read on into these poems, you will see a portion of all the things the Lord has revealed to me. They can make you think and wonder or even prompt you in longing to find the intrinsic spiritual truth of the Word of God and His kingdom. If you cannot understand or are offended by some of my writings, I pray that the light of the Lord above enlighten you, for I have written these from the depth of my heart; nevertheless, I say, "May His will be done."

Some of my poems are in parables, which have deep spiritual truth and meanings that I cannot fully express in poetry. To the last chapters, you will find that, although some are written about people and places, God has never been left out of the scene, because when I see creation, I see the Creator. And when I see the world, I see the Word that created it.

The Subject of This Book

Anyone who believes that there is a God who created and made this world—and knows we have a destiny after we cease from this mortal and earthly life—is running a race. As we know that in earthly races, there can be rival competitors, along with hurdles and obstacles that have been purposely placed by those who are hosting the race, depending on the type of competition. And it is at the hands of the athlete to master and overcome those hurdles and obstacles in order to finish the race and be qualified. The athlete cannot complain or grumble about those obstacles on the track. Or an athlete cannot give excuses saying they are too hard or too big to overcome. He or she has no choice but to learn to overcome them in order to finish the competition with the chance of becoming a winner. Though at times he or she may fail, that is only a lesson to learn from. And the next time, he or she will do much better and may even triumph over it, winning a prize.

When God reveals to you the truth about who He is and who you are, you shall find that, in the reality of the spirit, there are no enemies; therefore, there are no battles to be fought. Christ has won every battle for us on the cross. Your real enemy of success is you. You have to defeat you yourself because of unbelief and doubt that you cannot succeed in overcoming them. Those difficulties are part of the whole plan of God for your refinement—like gold through the fire—before entering heaven. If He had known that you are not capable of overcoming those difficulties, He would not let you face them, but because He allows you to face them, it is a clear sign that you can overcome them. Always remember God's promise, which says that He cannot let you be tempted and tested beyond your own strength and ability. And only through those difficulties you go through will you be defined as worthy to receive the prize as a winner in this race to eternal life.

Satan is no problem if we know the perfect will of God in creating him. Other people or things are not the problem if we know God's genuine purpose of creating them as well. Whatever difficulty and problem you have or will be going through is by the will of the master of the race, something you must never forget.

Please be aware that, whenever a person begins to grumble, grouse and blame other people or Satan for any tribulation or difficult situation encountered, the same is actually cursing the master of this spiritual race. I pray that you may come to this amazing light of the truth of God, and may you see that He is in full control of both the kingdom of light and life, and the kingdom of darkness and death as He has declared: "I am he that liveth, and was dead; and, behold, I am alive for evermore, Amen; and have the keys of hell and of death (Rev 1:18, KJV)." It is something that multitudes have failed to understand for ages, but now God is revealing it to us on this dispensation of time according to His own plan and prophesy.

Now listen. To blame others or Satan for any tribulations, failures and difficulties in life is only a repetition of the sin that our first parents committed in the garden of Eden. When the Lord God confronted Adam of his failure in obeying and keeping the command not to eat the fruit of the forbidden tree, he blamed Eve. And when He asked the woman, she blamed the serpent. No one was willing to own up to the problem. Everyone began pointing fingers at each other. In doing so, the Lord God's anger rose, and He pronounced His curse, beginning with the serpent, then to the woman, and finally ending with the earth for the man's sake. These curses were all because of one thing: blaming somebody or something else for the consequences of your actions and choices in life.

The attitude of blaming other people or Satan for any difficulties and failures you face in life brings the curse of God upon you. Therefore, never blame someone or something else or Satan for what happens to you, for it is according to perfect will of God, the potter. Lo, failure calls for perseverance to advancement. And difficulties are recesses of success.

Let me show you a few examples. If the evil people had not crucified the Lord Jesus Christ, we would not have eternal life. This eternal life and salvation that we know of and longed for became available to us only after His death on the cross. These evil men, by the will of God, made possible salvation and life to all humanity yesterday, today, and forever by crucifying Jesus the Christ, the Lord of Glory.

And if the Lord Himself during the Last Supper had not chosen Judas to betray Him, no one would be able to put his or her hand on this master of the universe. Many have tried to do so earlier on but did not. Yet when the time was ripe, He Himself gave the green light for the world to lay hands on Him. And by His own word, Satan acted through Judas to betray Him with a kiss. These are all found in an astounding enigma called "The Mystery of Wickedness" still at work today.

God is not foolish to create everything seen and unseen, good and evil, with no use at all. He created everything according to His plan and for a purpose. Good has a good purpose; evil also has a good purpose in Him. Blessed be His holy name.

As you come to the light of this said mystery, you shall be set free from worrying about any toothless and powerless enemy that has been haunting the lives and thoughts of every Christian and believer for generations. Only believe and you shall receive victory. If only you shall see things this way, you will find evil, Satan, and the devil as nothing to worry about and as if they do not exist. Yet they are there to make you become champions of life, and even the angels will stand in awe, seeing you run over any problem you may face in life. Just don't take the law into your own hands, but with hope, wait upon God, with love, repay evil with good, and, by faith, see that you have won the race. You can do it by mastering yourself in good times and bad, accepting everything you come upon, for they are there to make you becoming a victor, a champion, and an ace of this race.

The Outline of This Book

The first chapters of this book occasionally talk about how we must give our life to God, not necessarily using worldly materials, as the gift of Cain, Abel's brother. It also conveys the message of what lies behind the curtains of heaven that we are ignorant of because we rely too much on our church leaders for enlightenment and revelation, neglecting the promise of this new covenant that Christ has signed with His precious blood.

You might be aware or not that the Bible—from Genesis to Revelation—is a parable and blueprint. Those things that were written down did really happen, but in the spirit, they are pictures and symbols of the spiritual race every believer is undertaking to reach the Promised Land, which is eternal life. Remember that God is Spirit, and whenever He opens His mouth, He speaks of spiritual things in parables using the natural things. And we all believe that the Bible itself is the Word from God. And so it is written, "Give ear, O my people, to my law: incline your ears to the words of my mouth. I will open my mouth in a parable: I will utter dark sayings of old (Ps. 78:1–2, KJV).

My Appeal

Therefore, my beloved, we are living in an exciting and favorable day of the Lord. It is my earnest desire and prayer that whoever has gotten hold of this book and has a longing and yearning for God to know His depths, truth, ancient ways, and mysterious acts seize this opportunity and take another step to another level into this new way of life, a covenant written by the finger of God. This covenant is written no more in black and white, but of red and white, a living epistle, a walking Bible.

Christ's life will be your plus and class as you take on this adventure to the land of eternal living after victoriously triumphing this race to the finishing line where the Father and great cloud of witnesses awaits you, cheering you home. You shall not lack, for the Holy Spirit will be your depth and elucidation from this world's biggest parable book called the Bible. Hey! The same is the map—and the mind of the ace—of this race.

*And ye shall know the truth, and the truth
shall make you free* (John 8:32, KJV).

*If the Son therefore shall make you free,
ye shall be free indeed* (John 8:36, KJV).

Oh, my beloved,
may you run your own race,
and then you shall see His face.

So you just reach out,
with your whole heart—
not with your senses or any kind—
and then you will have His mind.

You will never be disappointed
because you are His appointment.

Christ shall take out that veil.
He shall be rid of that pall
from the face of this Moses,
and you shall see Him as He is,
know Him as He is,
and, therefore, live as He wills.

May you be blessed indeed,
seeing into the deep,
and reap,
and keep,
and give.

CHAPTER 1:

Symbolic

A Parable of the Gospel

On that day called Today,
I looked into the depths of His darkness
and heard a lion roar
with a voice like raging thunder,
standing on a balcony of gold.

And its roar echoed memorably
further back into time,
to the very ends of history,
even unto the day of the beginnings.

It spoke about the past generations
of the one who has the white robe.
And this beast was clothed with another robe
bearing the color of kings:
Hail, The reign of our God.

Then a man came along,
walking down from the ether
on an avenue filled with stars,
whose face shone like lightning,
dressed in a white robe
with the brilliance of the midday sun.

And his voice echoed intrinsically
further into the future,
even to the end of the week
unto today's generation.

His voice was so gracious and heart-tending,
speaking the words of mastery
and about the will of the one
who wore the purple robe:
Lo, the righteousness of our God.

After that, a ram proceeded out of the altar
that was made of bronze
and has the seven lampstands of gold,
staggering forth on a corridor of brass.

Its voice was like someone in agony,
speaking about the works Moriah and Calvary,
to put an end to the law of sin and death,
and the commandment must be laid to rest:
Behold, the sacrifice of our God.

Finally, I saw an eagle fly in
out of the depths of the beginning.
Its eyes were piercing through a veil of clouds,
and its wings were making a melody
touching and melting the cores of the daring hearts.

And when I heard it, I could not hold but tears.
Its voice came forth of its mouth
in the color of blue innately,
speaking in an ancient and mysterious tongue,
unveiling the things unknown, the dark sayings of old
of He who is the Most High:
In awe, I said, "The truth of our God."

The Bays of Days

First day passed:
Came forth he out of the past.

Second day passed:
Game forth he into the dust.

Third day passed:
Went forth he into his slavery.

Fourth day passed:
Light came forth into his tragedy.

Fifth day passed:
Left behind him to fend for himself.

Sixth day passed:
Left alone was he the end of himself.

Seventh day comes:
Eternity at hand to his new self.

Timetable of the Invisible

Day zero waited:
Everything stayed,
Beginning of this maze,
Ending with the big bang.

Day one came:
Blueprint was laid,
Beginning of the game,
Ending with them failed.

Day two came:
The lives were paid,
Beginning of a new day,
Ending with multitudes dead.

Day three came:
He became enslaved,
Beginning of the journey,
Ending with multitudes slain.

Day four came:
The price was paid,
Beginning at the hay,
Ending with Him dead.

Day five came:
Many more became baits,
Beginning with him burned,
Ending for many decades.

Day six came:
They seem to be deaf,
Beginning of her death,
Ending just yesterday.

Day seven comes:
A time for him made,
Blueprint is portrayed,
Ending with the end.

Then eternity comes:
Time is no more,
Beginning with zero,
Ending is no more.

The Cross in the Garden

O, how can I explain this,
for truth is not so plain?
This tree with two twigs:
the knowledge to riches
and knowledge to darkness.
Lo, the Tree of Understanding, the shrub's
clear standing, of God and humanity, about
their divinity and deity. Now I can see this: a
tree that is three, but one can never be free.
That sums up all to four and *death* is its very
core. I see the cross of Eden in the garden of
Gethsemane. And you ancient garden, you
will be there yet to the end.

Right there from the start,
thriving there in the dark,
a river flows and does part
irrigating the garden park.
Even the tree that is three,
but one can never be free.
Put up by God who is three,
but one is He that is indeed.
Yeah! Oh, the cross of Eden
you were there since then.
Still you remain hidden
from the glimpse of men.
Oh, the truth about thee,
thou art the shrub of Calvary.
And if a man must die on thee,
he shall make the choice unto eternity.

One Government, Two Covenants

I. The Contrasts

The old covenant was a figurative speech,
but this new covenant is a word of revelation.
The first covenant was a natural story,
but this last covenant is a spiritual reality.
The former covenant was symbolic outline,
but this latter covenant is the reality of life.
The earlier covenant was written with ink,
but this succeeding covenant is written by the Spirit.
The forerunning covenant was glorious at its appearing,
but this concluding covenant excels in glory in this end.
Yesterday's covenant ruled from without a man,
but today's covenant reigns from within a person.

The previous covenant was written on tablets of stone,
while this final covenant is written on
tables of the human heart.

II. Temples of Worship

Man made his temples
by his fingers and machinery
equipped with tools and utensils,
such as the hammer and emery.
And he uses worldly materials
such as wood and masonry,
which are all nonliving matters,
so this is a nonliving sanctuary.

God made His personal temple.
He made the man in mastery.
He had no tools and utensils,
yet He made the man wonderfully.
He cast the man from soil
and breathed the life unto the clay
so this dirt became His pearl,
grandly His living sanctuary.

III. Communion and Communication

Before, God was far-off.
He could not commune with men.
Only the pastors shall take care of
these many people as the shepherd of them.
Men did not know who God was.
They did not know God's manner.
They were there to receive a payoff,
so they did not know their Maker.

Today, God is not so far-off.
He is close to commune with men.
Anyone can partake of Him.
There's no need for a shepherd or a man.
Holy Spirit is the pastor there is
so everyone can know God's manner.
He is secret of the Father above.
Therefore, men can now know their Maker.

IV. The Epistles

The former letter was on stone tables
inscribed unto dead matter
with the purpose to be a parable.
And the veil remains as its cover.
This covenant was made to fleshy tables,
awaiting the coming of the latter,
which was revealed at His coming by the angels
when they cheerily announced the banner.

The latter letter is now on heart tablets
engraved onto these living organs,
the revelation of the parable.
Now Christ removes the curtains.
This covenant is the real label,
symbolized by the former picture,
which was revealed at His coming by the angels
when they merrily announced the banner.

V. The Last Day, The Seventh Day

Day of rest was on a week's last day,
according to the law of the works of men.
It was given a name as the day of rest,
a day of relief from all works of men.

It was given as a remembrance day.
No works shall be done on it by men,
a commandment until this very day,
yet the Sabbath remains a parable to men.

Today is the week's last day,
according to the law of the works of God.
The name is called the Sabbath day,
the day of the rest for every men.
It is no remembrance day at all,
for the Lord makes everything happen.
If you have heard of the Lord's day,
then count from Adam to this moment.

VI. The Reprise

A thousand years is as one day.
Don't be ignorant of this, o brethren,
a mystery you must never lay away,
or you might miss the promise again.
Jesus lived on this week's fourth day.
We are living on the third day from then.
His body is risen today
from the grave for to reign.

One day is a thousand years.
Don't be blind to this, o brethren,
a mystery you must never throw away,
or you will miss the *ark of rest* again.
This is the day called *Today*.
It is the day of the Lord.
Man was formed on this day.
We have arrived at that instant.

One Mystery, Two Ministries

Live by the law
and transgress the law.
Live by the Spirit
and fulfill the law.

Live by the law
and you are a seed of Cain.
Live by the Spirit
and you are a son of Abel.

Live by the law
and you are of Adam the First.
Live by the Spirit
and you are of Adam the Last.

Live by the law
and you are born of Hagar.
Live by the Spirit
and you are begotten of Sarah.

Live by the law
and you are a citizen of Egypt.
Live by the Spirit
and you are a resident of the Promised Land.

Live by the law
and you are not of Canaan.
Live by the Spirit
and you are neither of Egypt.

Live by the law
and live in bondage.
Live by the Spirit
and live a free age.

Live by the law
and live in slavery.
Live by the Spirit
and live in mastery.

Live by the law
and abide in captivity.
Live by the Spirit
and you are in liberty.

Live by the law
and you are destined to doom.
Live by the Spirit
and abide in freedom.

Live by the law
and pay the penalty of the law.
Live by the Spirit
and Christ is the penalty of the law.

Live by the law
and death is your destiny.
Live by the Spirit
and be in heaven's custody.

Live by the law
and suffer the wrath of God.
Live by the Spirit
and capture the favor of the Lord.

Live by the law
and live by which is ink.
Live by the Spirit
and live by the heart.

Live by the law
and you will not rest.
Live by the Spirit
and live on the crest.

Live by the law
and drink from Jacob's well.
Live by the Spirit
and drink from Christ's well.

Live by the law
and eat manna.
Live by the Spirit
and eat the answer.

Live by the law
and partake of the question.
Live by the Spirit
and eat of the truth.

Live by the law
and eat from the dust.
Live by the Spirit
and eat from above.

Live by the law
and eat from man.
Live by the Spirit
and partake from the holy One.

Live by the law
and you are of *possession*.
Live by the Spirit
and you are of *vanity*.

Live by the law
and the world becomes your dear friend.
Live by the Spirit
and the Lord becomes your best friend.

Live by the law
and God shall be your enemy.
Live by the Spirit
and the world becomes your enemy.

Live by the law
and debt is your wage.
Live by the Spirit
and your reward is grace.

Live by the law
and know sin.
Live by the Spirit
and know righteousness.

Live by the law
and live by sight.
Live by the Spirit
and live by faith.

Live by the law
and be vulnerable to corruption.
Live by the Spirit
and be impermeable to corruption.

Live by the law
and be condemned by the law.
Live by the Spirit
and you are free from the law.

Live by the law
and you are amenable to sin.
Live by the Spirit
and you are unable to sin.

Live by the law
and be an enemy of the law.
Live by the Spirit
and be a friend of the law.

Live by the law
and it becomes your foe.
Live by the Spirit
and Christ becomes your core.

Live by the law
and do the works of the law.
Live by the Spirit
and do the works of Lord.

Live by the law
and die by the law.
Live by the Spirit
and live to the law.

The Adams

The first was of the dust;
the latter is the Spirit.
The first was a mask;
the second is reality.

The former was created,
the masterpiece of all beings.
The last is the Creator,
the mastermind of all things.

The first is mortal,
the picture of the invisible.
The second is eternal,
a depiction of the invisible.

The mortal was given life
by the One who is life.
The immortal gave His life
to save the man that he can live.

The first came to be on the Sabbath
to keep and reap of this Eden,
commanded by the Lord of the Sabbath
to be the master of this garden.

The former was formed
by the One who was and is
so he can be conformed
to the will of who was and is.

The Duo

As the duo went their way,
they talked that one should stay,
but no one was willing to say,
so they arrived at *rolled away*.

Then they came to the house of God,
to the place of Elohim,
but the servant was not going to kneel,
so they went on from that hill.

They came to *humility*,
a town of humanity.
His master told him to stay,
yet he refused to be frail.

River *death* waited for them
as they reached their final destiny,
and there Elias was taken away
by the chariots of heaven,
never to be seen again.

Similitude

Just as the life of the man
has its source in the Lord God,
the life of the woman
has its source in the man.
And just as the Lord God
gave breath to the man,
the man gave life to the woman.

The man was formed
from a nonliving material,
but the woman was made
from living substances.

The man was made
before every occupants of Eden,
but the woman was the last
of all makes of the garden.

And as the life of the man
is found in the Lord God,
the life of the woman
is found in the man.

As the life of the woman
is derived from the man,
the life of the man
is derived from the Lord God.

The man got his life
directly from the Lord God,
while the woman got her life
indirectly from the Lord God.

And in resemblance to that—
as the Spirit has made known unto us—
I can say:

Just as the life of the church
is of Christ,
the life of the wife
is of the husband.

And as the head of the church
is Christ,
the head of the woman
is the man.

And just as Christ
is the husband of the church,
let the man
be husband of the woman.

As the church is subject
unto Christ in everything,
the woman must be subject
to the man in all things.

And just as the church
submits to Christ,
must the woman
unto her husband.

Peter Baibai

Just as Christ loves the church,
must the man love his wife.

And just as the church
is prepared for Christ,
the woman
was prepared for the man.

And just as Christ
is the Savior of the church,
the man died
to give life to the woman.

And just as Christ
died and rose for the church,
the man
died and rose for the woman.

Just as Christ
is the fullness of the Father,
the man
is the image and glory of God.

As the church
shares the glory of Christ,
the woman
is the glory of man.

And so as Christ
is not of the church,
the man
is not of the woman.

But if the church is of Christ,
the woman is of the man.
Just as Christ was before the church,
the man was before the woman.

Christ created the church for himself,
and the man named the woman himself.

The Offering (Part I)

Kayin, the subsistence farmer,
worked the *soil,*
laboring and toiling out his guts,
but *blood* was missing
in all his crops and veggies.

Hebhel, the keeper of his flock,
worked the *flesh*,
laboring and toiling with his heart.
Blood was pleasing
in all his cares and virtues.

When the time was ripe,
in the process of time,
Kayin gave his first fruit
to the master farmer,

but he was rejected,
for *blood* was absent.

And the time was right
at the end of the days,
Hebhel gave his first birth
to the master keeper.
He was accepted
'cause *blood* was present.

Kayin was downcast.
He was despondent.
Where did I go wrong?
He sought revenge,
the first murder record.

Hebhel was a custom.
He was complimented.
Way of the strong!
He got the acceptance,
the first tender record.

It must be a mystery.
Kayin gave matter
of this crude world,
so he was rejected
and given the mark
as a punishment.

In obscurity,
Hebhel gave his first life
so he was accepted
and given a mark,

a child of God,
as a compliment.

The label goes on
to the end of the week,
even today.
Choose you this day
what you would give
and please the Father.

Certainly,
there are Cains
and also Abels
living in the last day,
which is today.

So choose you this day.
What you would give
and please the Maker?

The Offering (Part II)

There sits the ultimate offering
for all humanity's wrongdoing.
This is a high time,
a remarkable moment
of what each man prime
concerning religious morality.

They stood up in array,
as if they owned this bay,
and thought this was okay,
as if God approved this way.

Yet there was also
this certain poor widow
with hardly anything to sow,
this old woman of low.

The Master looked on
as the rich moved on.
They all went onward,
giving what they had formulated
by their hollow decrees
and by power and greed.

Wow, they gave so much money,
but she gave just two mites.
They gave from abundance,
but she gave from her guts.
They gave from superfluity,
but she gave from her penury.

They gave a division.
She gave it whole.
They offered a fraction.
She gave not a portion.
They gave with their heads.
She gave her heart.
They gave much silver.
She gave much lesser.

The Word spoke up,
and the verdict was put up
by the one who is the Master
as He stood up to utter
the Word of His manner.

The Offering (Part III)

Lo, here is the mystery
in this sanctuary,
right here before the treasury.
At this time in the temple,
here at the synagogue
before the Most High God.

A recurrence came of the event
before who was in the beginning,
the witness of Kayin and Hebhel,
now sited in our midst
right before our very eyes.

The day of preference is here.
The day of favor of Lord is near
as blueprint repeats itself,
just as in the beginning.
The Lord spoke up,
only to their surprise
and to their astonishment.

Her gift was more than them all.
Her gift subdued them all.
Her offering exceeded theirs in all.
Hers surpassed theirs being put together.
During a time of favor from the Lord,
she offered more than them all.
She gave just a penny worth.
Invisibly, she gave not a penny worth.

Nothing of this matter world
is acceptable by the law of works,
which she brought to the Word.
'Twas not money that she gave.
Neither was gold that she offered.
Nor was silver that she brought forth.

They were tillers of the soil,
minding the things of this world.
She, a keeper of her flock,
was a pleasure to the Lord.

Her very life she gave.
Her very nature she gave,
back to the One who gave
and the One who saves.
It was here she gave
the firstlings of her flock,
her very first nature,
her very first birth,
her very old self.

And she was born again
into the kingdom of the Most High.
Be ignorant not, I beseech you,
for sin crouches at your door.
Be wise and give as she gave.

CHAPTER 2:

Life in God

The Mystery in God (Part I)

The life in God
Is a race without rivalry,
A competition without hostility.

For to be bound by Christ
Is true and perfect freedom.
And to be enslaved by Him
Is mastery and kingship.

The darkness in Him
Is the light of man.
And death in Him
Is life everlasting.

The poor and despised in Him
Are His treasure and pleasure.
And the lowly and folly in Him
Are His army and glory.

For what is hidden is the key,
And what He has revealed is the door
Unto freedom and wisdom of His kingdom.

The Mystery in God (Part II)

Lucifer: his habitation was heaven.
He was the melody of heaven.
His voice like a thousand angels,
more than I could angle.

Man: his habitation was Eden.
He was the warden of this garden.
His life was so noble,
even more than I could ponder.

The angel defied the Lord.
He desired the sides of the north.
Pride took hold of his core,
so he lost the fore.

The man transgressed the law.
He envied to be like the Lord.
Pride took hold of his heart,
so he was barred from this part.

He, angel of the morning, was expelled
from the mount of the congregation,
fallen from heaven
and the nations he had weakened.

He, a man of paradise, was dismissed.
He could no longer live in this bliss,
cast out to the earth
to return to the dirt.

And now on earth
they face each other.
Enmity is their theme,
and hostility is their game.
But their crime is the same!

The angel roves the planet,
making the sign of that plant,
and the man tends the earth,
wanting the fruit of that plant.

The angel accuses the man
before the God of man.
Man defies the devil
before the Lord of them.

I can only see
this rivalry scene,
but truth is what matters
about these two characters.

Listen to this.
There's something about these.
Open your mind
to pick up this sign.

"Why did you create man?" I asked.
"He's there for a purpose," the Lord answered.
I was so glad
'cause I'm not that bad.

"Why did you create Satan?" I asked.
"He's there for a purpose," the Lord answered.
I paused for a moment.
I could not comment.

"What? Shall we receive good at the hand of God,
and shall we not receive evil?" (Job 2:10, KJV).
"I form the light and create darkness:
I make peace and create evil:
I the LORD do all these things" (Isa. 45:7, KJV).

I found the answer
about this wonder,
that God had a purpose
of creating this person.

Must you know the truth
about this cherub,
for God is no fool
to create such a tool.

No trial and errors
in everything He renders,
for He is perfection
without imprecision.

All of existence
is without coincidence,
and every occasion
does have a reason.

Mastery in God

In Christ, you will face many crises.
But beyond the thickest darkness you've gone through,
You'll find the brightest light you've never seen.

Now behold!
In every circumstance,
God surrounds you.
And in every situation,
The Lord is stationed beside thee.
In every capacity,
Christ carries you.

And in every moment of time,
He leads you through a timeless life,
Reaching unto eternity
That is beyond humanity.

Therefore, you know
That faith is the price to pay.
Then righteousness will be the reward
And grace shall be the wage
From the One of all ages.

Life in the Lord

Life in the Lord is a competition without rivalry,
a competition not to whom would be the greatest,
but a race to who would be the least of all.
For by this shall a man venture
through the narrow gate
to eternity and live.

What shall I say then?
Climb down the valley
if you want to set foot on the mountaintop.
Come out of the *great house*
if you want to enter your inheritance.
And die to the self
if you wanna live
because life was not meant to be a trial
but to be lived.

For true riches are not often seen by others.
Neither is the world.
It is of the heart
manifested through the temple itself
by the mantle and the candle.
So it is the epistle of the inner man,
this letter of the Maker.
These can't be acquired in a flash.
Neither be obtained or attained overnight.
It is to be lived.

Behold, tomorrow is in the hands of today.
So be thankful and grateful for yesterday.
For working for yesterday is bondage,
but toiling for tomorrow is free-age.
Therefore, don't be found in the arena of debt
but in the field of investment.
Bestow today and live.

For today will never end until darkness comes
'cause it also began in the shadows.
And yesterday has passed away
when the man of clay was at rest,
for it also bloomed forth
when he was not aware of it.
So for the man are the days to live.

Therefore, to save time is to use time.
To taste time is to deplete it.
Voiding fulfillments is a waste.
Wisely use time as you live.

So see now, if one can quest,
what comes before the first
and occurs after the last?
What goes before the light
and comes after the night?
What happens before brightness,
and what appears after gloominess?
What exists before life,
and what is it the latter of death?

May the questions linger within
and be reasoned by the inner man.
So remember this—
man is a question
and the Lord is the answer.
Be wise and live.

Be Religious or Really Just

These can soften
or offend the prudent,
the lawyers and the teachers
of the law of works
and the nobles of Egypt.

Some can be confounded.
Others can be confused.
Numbers can be astounded
as numerous were astonished,
even provoked to revolt.

But the wise deride not
the words of the despised.
Therefore, don`t be religious,
but be really-just.

Entry by Humility

O, the angel poetry, even song.
Heaven was his habitation.
In heaven was his vocation.
But because of pride,
he took the ride.

Now it stands as an instance
that whoever dares to enter the entrance
of heaven's doors do the reverse
of Lucifer's mores.

What is the key to enter therein,
to the place of Him, where angels sing?

The poem is humility
and charity of his country.

Sweet Holy Spirit

The Holy Spirit is here to stay
to help those who will to pay
and give their life to the Master
to be led by Him in all matters.

He is the Holy One of God,
the sweetest person of God,
the keeper of the Father's secrets,
the treasure of the Father's mysteries.

No other like Him is here,
the One who is so dear.
Oh, how I long to be His best friend
and yearn to be my earnest trend.

How beautiful is my God,
and how wonderful is my Lord.
Yesterday was in His ways.
Today is in His caring hands,
and tomorrow is in His loving arms.

I will never be disappointed
for He is my appointment
and He is my covenant.
Now I rest assured
for He is my confidant,
and lo, He is my existence.

Until the end of my journey,
when I shall see my destiny
with Him my eternity.

CHAPTER 3:

Messages

.

Expect the Unexpected

Wow, heaven!
The home of the unexpected,
not for churchgoers
but for will-doers.

And now, hell!
The place of the unexpected,
not for will-doers,
but for transgressors.

One can say that he is of God,
and one can claim belonging to the Lord,
according to what has been written,
but the final verdict shall be
how one lives according His will.

Therefore, when church doesn't matter
and love becomes the only matter,
faith becomes His pleasure.
His will is the only measure.

Something you might not expect
and somewhat you might not suspect,
heaven is the home of the unexpected,
and hell too is the place of the unexpected.

The Seventh-Day Don'ts

Beware of the last,
the light of your *rest*.

ONE: Shall you not go out,
for there shall be none.
Empty shall you return.
Void shall be your reward.
Yeah! And emptiness shall be your wage.
Transgression to our God.

TWO: Buy not any victuals,
for that is not food.
A minute shall it last,
and the worms are at the bay.
O, and the stench of all that,
a defiance to our God.

THREE: Purchase not the fine wares
sold at your gates.
They're all but past due.
Naked shall you remain
and a shame of humanity,
an indignity to our God.

FOUR: Kindle not a fire,
least you should start
the anger of the Lord,
which cannot be quenched.
Your judgment you have incited,
a verdict of our God.

FIVE: Never leave your dwelling
and you shall be fed
with fare that is good
and eternity shall it last.
Have faith in our God.

SIX: Pray and seek Him not in the light of men,
as the dogs out in the streets
and hypocrites out on the byway.
But be as a couple in the secret place
with your husband the invisible,
and the fruits shall be the evidence.

SEVEN: Beware, Moses shall not be the letter,
neither the tablet be seen by men
as hypocrites out on the high way.
Truth shall be revealed in secrecy
by your husband the invisible,
and now the letter shall be in red and white.

The Word of God

The Word of God is truth.
It is the mind of God.
It's not bound by thought
And which cannot be due.

The Word of God saves.
It is the mind of faith
And not bound by death.
It cannot leave you in dire fate.

The Word of God is food.
It feeds the spirit of men
With an essence of heaven.
The Word of God is good.

The Word of God is the light.
It shines on the path of man
So this road can be fun
In this darkest night.

The Word of God is pure.
It does not have any grime.
Neither does it have any stain.
It can keep one secure.

The Word of God is holy.
It is the breath of the Lord
And brings all who dares to God.
The Word of God is wholly.

The Word of God is just.
It frees the soul of one
And shows the way to the son.
It diverts man away from the dust.

The Word of God is faithful.
It can never fail anyone
'Cause it is for everyone.
It fills all who dares to brimful.

The Word of God is His mind
Of how He wants us to be
And live the life that one should be
So we can be His kind.

Love is the Word of God
Manifested through His seed
Who came down to us beneath
With life that is so good.

The Word of God is the sword.
It cuts the deep asunder.
The cores of man be yonder
And binds the heart with accord.

The Word of God strengthens.
With care, it suckles the soul.
To the crest, it fills the bowl.
In Christ, we will heighten.

The Bread, My Breath

Blessed is He who comes from above.
Blessed is He, the bread of heaven.
Blessed is He, the breath from heaven.
And blessed is the man who draws from above.

Can men gather it from the face of the dust,
or can one amass it from the face of the dirt?
Can a man draw it from the wells of clay,
or can one fetch it from a man of mud?

Behold! There are multitudes
of wells that men have dug,
and there are magnitudes
of works that men have done.

But Moses's face is covered
with the veil of blindness.
His face is obscured
by the pall of sightlessness.

Where is it found then,
and what is its sound?
What is the noun
of the bread from the mount?

It is He who comes from above.
It is He, the bread of heaven.
He is the answer I love.
Christ Jesus, my breath even.

Knowing God,
Knowing Others

Knowing the Creator leads to knowing creation,
so seek the Creator to know creation.

Knowing God means knowing others,
and not to know God is blindness.

Now! You can never truly love your neighbor enough
until you come to the light of God's love for you.

You can never ever truly love God enough
until you truly see the light of God's love for you.

You can never ever truly know the mores of Satan
if you have never truly known the cores of God.

You can never ever really know yourself
if you had never ever truly known your God.

Until you see clearly the love of God for you,
you will never ever return His love for you.

Therefore, knowing the Creator leads to knowing creation,
so seek the Creator to know creation.

For knowing God leads to knowing others,
and not to know God is blindness.

Mercy and Love

To have mercy is to spare others,
and to love is to give in to others.

To receive mercy is not to pay the penalty,
but to love is to pay the full price of others.

To have mercy is having pity,
and to love is dying for others.

Mercy is given to the lowly, hopeless, and pitiful,
but love is given to the highly and enemy.

Mercy is the fulfillment to the doomed and damned,
as love is the accomplishment of the law and the prophets.

Mercy is given by the ruler to the poorer,
while love is given by the humble to the noble.

Mercy results in life of the receiver,
but love results in death of the giver.

Where there is no mercy, hopelessness prevails,
and where love is void, life is destroyed.

Mercy is given to the servants,
but love is given to the kings.

Mercy is given by kings,
but love is given by the least.

Mercy is given by the powerful,
yet love is given by the powerless.

Mercy is the work of kings,
while love is a deed of servants.

Mercy is in the power of masters,
but love is in the hands of servants.

Mercy is given from a throne,
while love is given from the dust.

Mercy is a king's service,
but love is a servant's duty.

A master has pity on his servant,
but a loving servant dies for his enemy.

Mercy gives hope to the helpless,
but love offers life to the enemy.

Mercy is required by the transgressor,
while love is acquired by the righteous.

Mercy is shown to the least,
while love is shown by the least.

Mercy delivers from judgment and condemnation,
as love liberates from sin and death.

Mercy delivers from penalty,
but love pays on behalf of penalty.

Mercy is by the wish of the receiver,
while love is by the free will of the giver.

Mercy offers relief to the wretched,
while love offers a cross to the giver thereof.

Mercy is given to dawn,
while love is needed at dusk.

Mercy flows from superiority,
but love streams out of humility.

Mercy results in forgiveness,
while love ends with obedience.

Mercy is the fulfillment of the masters,
as love is the completion of the commandments.

Mercy is the conclusion of forgiveness,
while love is the end of truthfulness.

Mercy delivers from condemnation,
as love liberates from punishment.

Mercy unleashes liberty,
while love is the fulfillment of the trinity.

Mercy is humanity,
and love is charity.

Mercy comes from a compassionate heart,
but love flows from a passionate heart.

Mercy opens the door to freedom,
and love unlocks the heart to wisdom.

Love and Fear

Those who fear men
do not fear God,
but those who fear God
shall not fear men.

He who belongs to the day
does not fear the night,
but those who belong to the night
fear the night.

He who belongs to the night fears men,
but he who belongs to the day fears God.

Love God, and the world will face you.
Fear God, and He'll save the world through you.

Fear the world and subdue to the world.
Fear God, and men will fear you.

Those who are afraid of the dark
do not belong to the light,
but those who belong to the light
fear not the dark.

Love the world, and you become
the world's best friend.
Love God, and the world
will not be your dread.

Please God, and thy enemy shall be
at peace with thee.
Please the world,
and put the world in jeopardy.
But love the Lord,
and save the world from its calamity.

The Heart, The Right Sight

Recalling the days of the traveler,
this man was a wanderer
from east to the west in that order,
even to the south of that count,
seeking which was not to be found
by any of these worldly bounds.

By the sea he went.
Air was the common lane.
The mammal, a weary trend
seeking him, which is invisible,
just like a hopeless puzzle.

Knowing not what he'd said afore,
senses are useless.
Matter is worthless.
The members are hopeless.

Peter Baibai

Yet when the time was set
cometh the day of deliverance
'cause of his persistence,
seeking the Lord as he can be,
just as he could be.

He found the heart, the Zion mount,
the only medium to the city of Him,
and found this gold who is the Lord.

This ordained organ, this rightful pane
of the human temple, the acceptable.
And here he saw the miracle.

I See

I see this God.
I see the splendor.
I think of the Lord.
I am filled with wonder.

I see Adam.
I see a man of clay.
I think of Adam.
I think of the seventh day.

I see the man.
I see the header.
I behold a man.
I know a leader.

I see the woman.
I see a partner.
I have a woman.
I got a helper.

I see Noah.
I think of the Sabbath.
I think of Noah.
I know one's death.

I see Noah.
I am relieved.
I found this Noah.
I am at *rest*.

I see this Moses.
I see the shadow of the law.
I view this Moses.
I think of flaw.

I see Moses.
I know a fading covenant.
When I see Moses,
I see disappointment.

I see *drawn forth*.
I think of corruption.
I see *drawn out*.
I found transgression.

I see Joshua.
I think of this warrior.
I hear this Joshua.
I know my Savior.

I see the cross.
I think of Job.
I see the cross.
I think of gross.

I see Peter.
I think of zeal.
I see Peter.
I think of the seal.

I see Joseph.
I know *another one.*
I see Joseph.
I think of the Mighty One.

I see Steven.
I think of the throne.
I think of Steven.
I cherish a crown.

I see the Sabbath.
I think of the last day.
When is the Sabbath?
I know it's today!

Know Now

Thou shall not fall prey.
At least thou shall not fall—I pray—
to the one of the night,
to the one on the right
of the Lord of Hosts, the Commander
standing in the fore of the Father.

There was the voice I heard,
the tone of this, my shepherd
saying which was being said
about the manner of this quest
because this road is so dimmed,
yet the lamb shall be thy lamp.

Cease all the go
and end all the flow.
All these are options of vanity
and courses of iniquity.

Thy money shall perish with thee
if thou hast thought that way.
Flee from the abominable sin,
thus the gall of bitterness
and bond of iniquity.
Neither a place is to be found
under this very sun.
Nor any decibels can be heard
from the Holy One of God.

So be wise and seek Him.
Be nice to court Him.
Let you be a pleasure to Him,
and you shall be nurtured by Him,
for your future shall be with Him.

A Memo

On this dirt,
on this earth,
believe to live,
and have faith to gain.

Hope is a future tense,
Faith is a present tense;
Love is the present continuous,
and the past holds handy lessons.

Must you remember this
that the world is a crisis,
but you ought to be wise
'cause these crises
can be your genesis.

Though at times will you thirst,
but stand firm to be first.
Be a knight in this night,
and you shall fight for your right.
For the gospel, do the work,
and be rewarded for your worth.
Yet be sober in the order
of the holy and the wholly
which are of God and not of Gog.

So know the trade of your make
and the version of your mission.
Do not slumber as the lumber,
but be vigilant with your talent.

Be strong and don't go wrong
as a pier and not be dire.
Never fear, for you're so dear
to the One whose more than one
against the adversary and the enemy.

For the Lord is your ford,
turning impossible to potential
and nonviable to a miracle,
turning all nights into light.
By His might, you shall do right,
for you have His mantle in this battle.

So be wise and not be vice,
for your ministry is charity.
And your calling is not of frowning,
neither of grumbling but of trembling
with fear while you are here.

Thy reward is being prepared,
for your price is the Christ
and the wage is at His gate.
You shall see it when you take your seat
in the land of wonder in the home upper.
So be it in the ether.

Chapter 4:

Testimonies

The End of Nothingness

When the earth was without form,
the Spirit of God was the only sum.
And when the earth was yet nothing,
darkness was the only thing.

In the cradle of the unknown,
He existed on His own.
His dwelling was the face of the waters
behind the deep well of the darkness.

When time was yet asleep,
the Spirit was the only keep.
And when matter was yet absent,
God was the only substance.

When beginning was yet nothing
and when the morning was yet hiding,
He nurtured His plan of the future,
just like a woman preceding labor.

Then He sent forth His Word,
and there came forth the worlds.
By His Word, the universe was framed,
and it bloomed forth into its plane.

By faith, light burst out.
By His Word, light came about.
And when He opened His mouth to sing,
there occurred the big bang.

Peter Baibai

So all creation ceased from nothingness
and emerged into existence,
as the firmament became a vast vault
and the heavens became a grand mall.

My Testimony

Once I was lost,
Vice I did most.

Blind and bound for the tomb,
Kind of a noun to be doomed.

Tried so hard to gain His favor,
But nigh was the mud as my future.

Chaos was all I did seek.
Mess was all I had picked.

Muddle was all I sought.
And bubbles was all I fought.

Nowhere near was I to the Master.
Somewhere near was I to the gutter.

Trying to make it on my own,
Frying myself on the iron.

Ready for the feast of the beast,
Just for a meal was my best.

And what I have got onto my neck
Was not that yoke of His pack.

But then at His own will,
At the pleasure of His own bill.

Showed me His amazing grace,
At His own phase and case.

Came down to rescue me.
Game now I couldn't be.

Shed His blood for the remission,
For that was the stump of His mission.

So I am pronounced not guilty,
As the angels had announced my treaty.

This has made me free to subsist
So I can be in bondage to Christ.

To be His inheritance as His bride
And be His substance and His pride.

Unto the humility of His saints.
Oh, and the dignity that will paint.

So now I am privileged to live,
As now I have the knowledge to life.

In His courts, I will praise,
For this course I do raise
My hand to the holy one of God
And to the only Son of God.

And in the law of this Spirit,
I will do things right.

Shall I dwell in comfort therein,
And I will cherish His well herein.

So let my heart be His seat.
For this life, I have His zeal.

And my name will have His seal
In which I know is so real.

And to eternity, my life will be.
In immortality, my life shall be.

Once

My Jesus came down to us
to rid all men's sin once.
So He said this once
that love is what we should not do just once.

He gave His life for once,
and He paid the price just once.
But how can I say this once
'cause He is more than one?

My Jesus left this with us
that we ought to be wise.
It is to us, a must,
least we might bust.

*Now there will be signs
of when that day comes,
when I will return at once.
So be ready for that at all times.*

The Adulteress

Condemned woman
By the law of men
Was caught in the act with another man
In breach of the law of man.

Was worthy to die by the law.
Brought her they to the Lord
To see what He would say.
Must the woman have to pay?

The Master stooped down wordless.
They waited with eagerness
That He may say His word,
Only to tempt the Word.

Pestered the more them from Him.
Stood up Him and answered the team,
Who has never done crime
May lob the first at this one!

Inaudibly, they all scattered,
For their plan was shattered.
Like ghosts, they dispersed.
And as if they had wings, they disappeared.

From the religious front men
To the commoners who came,
All of them—they—went,
Not one of them was left.

One way, they came forth.
In seven ways, they all fled.
These aces of the law
Were caught up in their own law,
Messed up by their own flaw.

The Lord lifted and said this:
Where are your accusers?
No man, Lord,
She said to Him.

The Law from above spake this:
Neither do I condemn thee:
Go, and no more, shall thou sin.

I Woke Up

I woke up this morning
and found that I am alive.
What can I say about Him?
He is the reason I'm a life.

How can I voice this?
No words I can find
since He's more than bliss,
even more than this mind.

In the pulpit shall He know
for it is His dwelling,
the essence and His home,
and the source of our telling.

Peter Baibai

What gracious God we serve,
more than words we could say.
In righteousness, He serves
more than what we could play.

The Journey (Part I)

Go on, man of clay!
Start at the waters
and end at the tomb
if you dare eat honey.

Where meat becomes a fountain,
never fading with time,
and becomes a pleasure to the Father
who seeks such kind.

Where a babe is fed with milk
and a child lives as a king
And where the weak are giant slayers
and the fools are made of wisdom.

Go on, man of dust,
for the glory has become just a story
and the essentials have only become fables
in the dais of the church.

Fear of death reigns in their hearts
without faith to go that far.
So they cease after a few nights
and miss the essence of all that.

But out of the waters of demise,
the Maker certifies a man,
as the end becomes a beginning
of the pilgrim who is wise.

Peter Baibai

Go on, man of the earth,
out of that comfort zone,
into the no-man's-land,
where the tempter awaits the mortal.

And you shall see this come to pass
when flesh melts down before your eyes,
as nature becomes your true witness
and the wild beasts will be your closest guests.

The Journey (Part II)

Twelve nights gone by.
A lesion in my leg ceases to be,
and the gash in my foot disappears,
but the lust of the stomach is so strong.

A pen in my hand,
the tablet before me,
and a jotter on my lap,
but the stringed instrument lay idle.

The wild fowls emerge from under the thicket.
The snail crawls onto my veil,
while the vultures draw nigh to melting flesh,
speaking in tongues that I could not understand.

The fire subsides anterior me,
as if dying slowly in this pitch blackness.
I could sense the presence of the company,
some come so close, touching this temple.

Sixteen nights gone by,
and the scent becomes so strong,
as tissue begins to thaw out slowly
and passes out as urine,
drying up the brush as herbicide.

The mouth is filled with foul stench,
as tissue in bloody form accumulates within.
The spittle of the mouth tastes like salt
and dries off as it leaves the tongue.

Peter Baibai

Wines and creepers about are dried up.
The plants and shrubs around turns pale,
while the wilderness is filled with
animation and boisterousness
in undefined tongues and fuss
as creatures of the wild gather.

Sweet, savory scents of restaurant foods
occasionally pass by from nowhere,
coming right past my nose in tempting offer.
So the belly's lust becomes so coercing,
so intense seems to be blowing my brain apart
with an appeal to go home.

For sure, this must come to pass.
This is the launching of test number one.
I could sense the presence of the angel
proportionally accumulating to time.

The serpent silently slinks in beside me
once, this four-footed beast of the field,
with an earnestly sullen face,
heeding attentively with its tongue,
but one thing I know for sure,
this is the arrival of the temper.

My strength begins to diminish gradually
after eighteen nights without victual.
The stringed instrument lies there forsaken,
and the pen is now jiggling between the fingers.

Wow! Then this hand reaches forth to fireplace
and moves the wood together again,
as a servant serving his master.
I could only see the angel's shadow.

Flesh continues to be liquidized,
living behind the framework, a human scaffold.
The lights at the window sink deeper into their dome,
and movement is now like a toddler learning to walk.

At dawn, a messenger turns up,
tells me certain specific things, and departs.
I wait for a confirmation from him
whether to carry on to the fourth week or not.

This was the third week when he came by.
The beasts and birds are closing in.
Evidently, vultures, snails, snakes, and
rats become bed companies,
waking up with them all over me,
yet the fear of them is gone.

The Journey (Part III)

The journey carries on yond
to where mortality begins,
the spiritual prison planet under heaven,
into Succoth and to Pi-hahiroth,
the place before the sea of blood.

We walked through the great wall of salty ice,
in the midst of the standing waters of reeds,
and emerged out a few miles just before the *land of bitterness*.
We passed the *acreage of the grumblers*
to the place of temptation and lusts,
where the Lord had sworn, waging war on them
from generation to generation.

Then we journeyed on to the *mount of the law*,
where carnality was brought to life
and sin became alive to slay every transgressor,
where death and sin kissed each other.

Again, we left for Taberah and Hazeroth,
where the woman entices the high priest to rebellion,
that place before Kadesh.
And here before our fore
was the place where only faith counts.

We turned and entered the wanderings
only to come face-to-face with Hor,
he who slew the man of God who rebelled
in coinciding with the woman,
against the one who is called "drawn out"
of the world's biggest river.

Again, we took to the king's highway,
passing Petra and the *home of the giants,*
through the land of the *red stuff* and lost heritage
until we came to the edge of the river of death.

There we passed through its grubby waters on dry ground
to the land where all burdens are being *rolled away* today.
Then we entered into the great city below the sea
where the three kings were crushed by the number of God.

From there, we proceeded to Ephraim,
where the choices were made by the chosen people.
And there is where the manmade bakery was instituted
by the one who has the *strength like God.*

Then we proceeded on to see the Prince of Salem
who lived in the city of Ariel.
And thus, we beheld the star of the *beloved.*
It is symmetrical, equal and balanced,
and appears same from all directions and in all seasons,
proclaiming to all mankind the full message of salvation
of Him who is the same yesterday, today, and forever.

The Journey (Part IV)

But back at the wild, the messenger's message came through
and confirmed my cessation of this mission.
So it was time to go back home,
calling off the journey to a later time (if God wills).
So I made a prayer with the beasts and hosts with me.

I said farewell to the wild and staggered slowly up the hill.
I had to take many breaks at every ten meters,
for the puissance and muscles were all gone.
Only the temple frames were grinding themselves
as I could feel within.

I turned and looked back from a fair distance.
Drops of liquid came out of the window,
for they had been my witnesses to this testimony
and so the Maker of all humanity.

CHAPTER 5:

People and Places

My Town Went Down

Oh, my town of volcano,
Now it's still filled with canoes,
Once the town of frangipani
Where my friends were so many.

Once my beauty Rabaul,
Now you can hardly be found.
Was charming before the blow
And was busy as people flow.

Once the place of mangroves,
Now a town of human hooves.
Now you, my Barike land,
Oh you, my barren land.

So beautiful with ash and dust,
Now wonderful as a mask,
For the dust so speaks
And the musk of larva streams.

I can only recall
The moment of that fall.
'Twas September nineteen ninety-four
When you spewed out your core.

Never did I ever see
Anything like that scene.
When the skies were as dark as noon,
Filled with rocks and debris so soon.

Ash was the only roof hovering,
Like the gloomy caves of *tunnel hill*.
Panic was the main event that date,
And movement was never paused 'til very late.

That was the bustle by your inhabitants that day
Till all were well away,
Out from the well of fear,
Unto covers not so near.

Oh, when the twin shattered my town
With a shuddering movement at dawn,
Just as it had been planned.
And so my Rabaul was banged.

It was like a stampede
By an army from deep beneath,
With a force so great that day,
Which words could not say.

'Twas the god of fire and the bee,
Like guns of fire from the deep.
Yet in God we will live.
In God we shall lean.

From Vulcan to Tavurvur,
I now can softly murmur
A wee whisper in your ear,
As if you could wish to hear.

Yet the thundering of the bee,
So deafening as it can be,
As if it could muff up my drums
As a cannon of military arms.

And the devastation of the god of fire,
So desolating and so dire,
As it buried up the villages
With an anger kept for ages.

And the smoke of the inner chambers
Rises more to the ethers,
As I stood there amazed
At His goodness to this age.

And no one did perish.
Only the assets were buried
More than fifteen feet under.
We would have been ashes as lumber.

When the twin hit the roof,
Only to leave behind a big groove
Of mud and destruction
And a mug of devastation.

As property in quantity
Vanished from sight so quickly,
That'll take time to rebuild or restore
Or even never and forever.

Shall it be as a gesture
And a signal of a picture
Of the page of His grace
At the glimpse of His face.

As I behold His glory in this time,
Which shall be a memory in this mind
That will never be fully erased
In this truly miraculous era.

So we can rest assured
That we can be cured
In His own phase
At His own pace.

As we enter His rest
At everyone's own crest,
According to one's own heart,
And eternity shall be our part.

Papua New Guinea (A Prophesy)

O, man with the beard,
You must have heard
The word of His favor
And the voice of His tenor.

O, man with the dreadlocks,
Won't you come out of that deadlock?
Come, grasp the time of your fulfillment
As the time reaches its fullness.

And you, o linguist,
Don't you know you are on His list?
You need to be conscious
To execute His counsel.

O, man with a multitude of tongues,
The nation with many speeches,
More than seven hundred I should say
On this seventh day.

Lying there at the far east,
Yet you have been the least.
All day you face the gate of the sun,
Trying to get a glimpse of the glory of the Son.

Do you know that His grandeur
Will come in from that door?
Hey, watcher of the Eastern gate,
It's not yet very late.

Only if you should awaken
From your sleepy condition
Because your new day is dawning
For you to cease your evening.

Know the word concerning thee,
For the finger is pointing at you.
O, man from the sunrise,
From the land of paradise.

You there, Sepik, do you ever think about this?
And you, Madang, do you ever see this?
To the highlander, do you work this out?
Hey, you Morobe, can you smell the fragrance?
The southern region, don't you see
that finger pointing at you?

Oro and Milne Bay, you have aged so greatly!
And New Britain, how long have you been asleep
In your mother's womb?

The full message hangs there on that pole daily,
Flying there before your very eyes,
Placed there by an ignorant one,
Only used by the omnipotent One.

Your dread hair hangs behind you,
And the finger points at you from beneath.
Only if you could know this
That you are the ravenous one from the east.
O, man from the land of the unexpected,
The man who speaks so many tongues,
The one from the land of paradise,
The man from the sunrise.

May you be subject
To the law of the anointed One.
Then the unction of the Holy One
Shall go with you and reap spoils.

Now that you are here,
Cease from all insensibility
And the paths of obstinacy,
For all these are just vanity.

To the glory of His kingdom,
You shall be a pillar of the temple,
For white linen shall be your mantle
And the color of kings shall you bear.

As the deep shall be your gold,
Scarlet shall be thy gift.
And placidity shall be thy heritage,
With the Maker of this mortal man.

Then thou shall rise as the morning,
And dawn shall be your resident
As evening vanishes before thee.

A fool to this world,
But wisdom shall be your vesture,
And knowledge shall be your garment.

You have been wanted
More than you have thought.
Now that you are informed,
Rise up and be conformed
To the will of Jerusalem,
To the voice of the Prince of Salem.

A Song of the Ocean

The coves, the whales, and waves,
the starfish and the jellyfish,
the weeds and the reefs,
the crab and the clam,
islands and atolls.

Turtles are reptiles.
Corals are animals.
And corals are floras.

Whales do not have scales,
and the dolphins do have big fins,
but the shark was never put in the ark.

An ocean is like a mansion of glory.
She is like a manor of shrubbery.
She covers the earth to two-thirds
and conveys the rhythm by her moving tides.

Oh, the beauty of the ocean as seen from mountains,
and the deity of the ocean has been there for eons.
She has pillars of the palace of her greatness
and a fortress and temple of all the fishes.
She's filled with treasures without measures,
where there are hills and valleys that she nurtures.
Yet there are ridges and mountains found within,
and there are masses of land that is known therein.

Oh, how thy depths lie unsearchable
and how thine keeps be immeasurable.
Who can gauge the beauty of thy inner vesture?
Mysterious and unknown is your inner chambers,
just like the master with many treasures.

Your shores display thy garment
just as the wind blows upon thy raiment,
vast as the wind rages in a violent movement.

For as the waves are the gestures of your scepter,
so are the coves the filters of thy breathers.
And as the fishes are assets of thy riches,
so are corals the floras of thy patches.

And as the creatures at diverse fill thy waters,
so it features the various lives of your borders.

See, the seas are daughters of thee,
just as the hive that houses the bees.
Yet I will always cherish thine splendor
as you sit there with thy order
that has caused me to wonder
of the mystery that is beyonder
about the One who is your Creator.

The River and the Fisher

A river is a giver
of water from its altar
in the fountains of the mountains,
flowing down like a gown
to the sea where I can see
past the rocks to the docks.

And on the river was a fisher
with his gun in the sun,
an endeavor without an answer.

Then he came by to his manner
and prayed softly to the Creator,
"At least a hand fuller."

So the Creator said to the water,
"Withheld not from the catcher!"
And so the fisher got what he asks per.

"Blessed art thou, oh fisher of the river,"
said the Maker to the hunter.
So the same went home much pleaser
and he parted on to his manor,
just as the river continued on its liner.

Children

Children are blessings from the Father,
which are brought forth beneath the ether.

They are reflections of the couples,
but let them not be troubles.

They are mirrors of the parents.
Seeing them, you see what the trees are like.

Children are fruits of the body,
growing up to be somebody.

They are results of secrecy
to behold obviously.

And they are beauties of marriage
and products of the aged.

Children are flowers of the home
and not to be left alone.

They are born to err
and to be led away from error.

So they should be groomed,
and they shall also be pruned,
as the giver has commanded
and as He has instructed.

A conscientious parent spends time with the children,
but a negligent father shall reap what he has sowed.
And the mother shall eat the fruit of tears of sorrow,
for a child left to himself brings a reproach to the father
and shall cause shame to the mother.

A disobedient child is a boor,
and a rogue is a misery and gloom
to the one who brings about such boon.

But an obedient child is bliss,
and a submissive child is wise.
The same shall also rise.

Children are delight to the parents,
for each has a kind of talent,
been dawning since yesterday.
It shall become clearer as the day.

And a prudent father is a guide,
and a practical mother shall be a model,
as shining stars in the darkest night.

So teach obedience to the child,
and you shall rest a while.
Teach them the way to go,
the path they should follow.

Speak fine words of inspiration,
good deeds of motivation
for the success in their motion
on their road to privilege
of getting hold of knowledge.

Treat the children as plants
of the garden in your front yard.
See that they blossom from the bottom
to the acme of their being.
Water them regularly
and nourish them frequently.
Sweep the clouds away from their faces
so they may reach into a clear sky.
And they may see at the end
of their venture, a bright sight,
at the end of the line, a goal mark.

And at the last chapter of their own book,
a beautiful ending says,

Blessed be the Father of my father,
and blessed be the Maker of my mother,
who was and is and will be forever.

Venture

The plane flew very high,
and it drew very nigh
to the clouds of the sky
with a loud, noisy cry.
Oh! And I wish I could fly.

And I'll soar right to the heavens
to see the world at its fullness
and see the beauty of its vastness.

Nevertheless, I'm comfortable.
By His life, I am able
to fulfill in this temple
and enjoy His approval
through His son, my miracle.

Now while we are still alive,
let each one live the life
that can yield us to thrive
in one's own hive.

To the end of this venture,
for it is our indenture
on this green pasture,
so let us not falter
and let us not waver.
Till we get to heaven
unto the garden of Eden
and the company of the chosen.
Amen.

A Tone of Names

Adam was the first man.
He was before all of them,
while Eve was the first bearer of life
and she was Adam's helping wife.

Cain was disdained
because his gift was in vain,
but Abel was the able
'cause his gift was acceptable.

Noah built the ark
in a dry land park,
and then the rain fell as grain
and covered up all the ground.

Abraham had a ram,
but then he was given a lamb,
and so Isaac was not sacrificed
because he was the sanctified.

Moses is full of many verses,
which are not just mere stories,
while Joshua is the savior
who keeps my life secure.

Miriam had this bitter name,
so she tried to overrule the game,
yet Moses was chosen
to lead the people and nation.

Jacob was like a jackal,
seizing a break to topple.
But Israel was the chosen child
preferred when he was running wild.

David was the beloved.
He had defied the opponent.
And Solomon was the uncommon,
for he had the spirit of wisdom.

Jezebel was a rebel.
Her husband could not tell.
Ahab was a mishap,
and his wife was a hacker.

While Vashti failed to see
her modest duty,
Esther took the order
and became the star.

Ruth was a friend who was true,
and her love for Naomi grew.
Even when asked to turn back,
she remained her friend's best.

When Ruth had borne her fruit,
a child of Boaz she had brought forth,
Naomi was so happy,
and she was very merry.

Mary was not prepared for marriage,
but heed unto the angel's message.
And Joseph was not that type,
so she, he could not discard.

Matthew could count a few,
for that was what he knew.
And John counted it all joy,
for he was His choice.

Paul became small
when he took that fall,
while Timothy was worthy
to become our missionary.

CHAPTER 6:

Concluding Poems

Sense

It is apparent that everything,
every thinking, has a contrary.
This is because everything
that exists has a distinct duty
to keep existence of all things
in balance and symmetrically.

Even though one can say
that there is no destiny of all things,
it does not alter the course of anything
because destiny itself exists: a word.

Even though one can say
that there is no life after death,
it does not alter the course of life and death
because life itself is the forerunner of death
and for a seed to die is the way to a new life.

Even though one can say
that there is no God,
it does not change God,
because He is unchangeable,
the same yesterday, today, and forever.

Even though you can say
that existence is coincidental,
it does not agree with existence,
for even your words do not come
from coincidence.

Song to the Backslider

Heaven rejoiced
when you made that choice
to take on this adventure
that'll determine your future.

You know you have been right
in choosing the light,
a choice and not a command
imposed by no one.
It was a free will
by your own deal.

You've seen how the life was
on this daring course.
It was not that easy
that one could be so lazy,

a life full of courage
and a road of persistence.

But the One who had called you
had been so good to you.
In all these years,
He had been so near.
He had been so faithful,
and you had been so joyful.
He had given you a privilege
so you can have a heritage.

Now you have turned away
from the One who is the way.
Heaven is disappointed
by the deed you have taken.
You've turned your back on the Master,
something hard for me to utter.

What was it that caused you to leave?
He was there when you took to leave,
stretching out His hand to you
so He could take over from you
to take away your quandary
and carry away your calamity.

Calling out your name gently,
telling you not to worry.
But you would not listen,
maybe you were not certain.
Only if you had believed,
you would have been relieved.

Yet you would not attend to Him,
and you would not listen to Him.
You turned away to go
as He stood there seeing you go.
Tears fell from His eyes,
rolling down to His cheeks,
like one who has lost a loved one,
whom He had been with for a long time.
He stood there looking as you went,
knowing the *free will* you have.

Now, it has been a long time
on His waiting for you to come,
trying to get a faint sign of you,
drying His face off the dew,
looking out at the horizon
in all these times and seasons.
Patiently, He is waiting.
Tenderly, He is calling
for you to come back …
for you to turn back.

Pardon and Strength (A Prayer)

Let my supplication come before thee, oh my God.
And my voice be heard in thy habitation, oh my Lord.
Do not be weary unto my request, oh my Answer.
Neither my call be nonsense to thee, oh my Master.
Nor my petition be considered sin
unto thee, oh my Redeemer.

Be merciful unto me, oh my justice,
According to your amazing grace,
And all you have bestowed on this
Through thy only Son Jesus Christ.

Search me and find in me
If there is any wicked way,
Pardon me and show me your way,
The path of thy verity
So I may abide in thee
And forevermore, I will be.

And thy truth be my light
To shine on my night
So I may live as You require
And doeth the things You desire
For Your glory to be seen
More than I have ever been.

Let You be my shepherd,
And only Your voice shall be heard
As I walk to my destiny
So I might not fall into iniquity.
And let me be a victor o'er the enemy.

And tomorrow will be bright
As I do things right
According to thy goodwill,
And without measure shall I dwell
In thy presence eternal
And looking back, not at all.

About the Poet

A poet is a poem.
And poetry is a beauty.
So this song can't be wrong
but a delight of my life.

Blessed be the mind that soars high,
like an eagle in the depth of the sky.
Understanding becomes a privilege,
and he becomes a high vantage.

This is a lover of that kingdom
and favor according to Him,
where lights never go out
and nights don't show up.

Where sorrows hide behind the Hades,
death never comes out of Sheol,
the stars never cease to shine,
and the moons never stop their orbit around the Son.

An admirer of the nature
and a lover of the future
yet has much to utter
but never a teacher.

A lover of this habitat
where there is no death,
lavishing the kind of riches,
can never be gotten by pretense.

Found not by most at any cost
but sincere and true courses,
so this is a measure of treasure
by the course of my indenture.

Deeming poetry as a gift
from Him who is the *gift*
to the yearning of the soul
for something behind that veil.

Lo, these poems are of life
and life that is so nice
from a life of observance
and a life of occurrence.

Pursued he into the deep,
living the life of his deeds,
what a beauty to understand
about the freedom at the end.

Yeah! What a privilege
to acquire such knowledge
of the things I love
from the One who is *love*.

The utterance of the narrative man
of his inner keeps hidden.
These verses are of an account,
and he's a version of this account.

Gratifying are the revelations,
which are not bound to imaginations,
deems poetry as a blessing
from the One whose deeds are blessings.

A light of love,
lamp of passion,
the thinker's mind,
and a dreamer's heart.

Can be offensive
but likely be incentive
to the reader, I mean,
but blessed be the keen.

Know the deep things of God,
so be bold and be strong.
This height so beautiful,
a class of love so wonderful.

Beholding creation's beauty
on this path to one's destiny.
May you grasp this wonder,
so shall you know what lies under.

To see what has been hidden
from your person within
for your own bookish page
in this coming age.

Alphabet Summary

Announcing the *rest* of our God.
n ark has been prepared to go.
nd the day has dawn.
ncient days, we are found.

Begotten Son of the Father.
estowed for the good of man.
etrothed to His church.
ehold! He cometh in the clouds.

Come let us enter by the way.
omfort is waiting.
ome before it is too late.
ommit thyself today.

Don't be so foolhardy.
o away with debauchery.
oor awaits your knock,
ock thyself on this rock.

Earnestness, be thou rise.
arly longing soul, be prized.
astern wall awaits the chosen,
ach spirits of Goshen.

Freedom waits beyond Nebo.
rom Gilgal beyond the Jordan ghetto.
railty, He has the balm.
riend, He's calling you to come.

Girdle up now to thy journey.
ifted morning, I should say.
iven at the mother's womb.
ive back to Him now at the tomb.

Heaven awaits, so why wait?
eaven's angels joy for this date.
earken the voice, the harmony.
eavier than air, it falls to earthlings.

In the midst of the waters, a salty wall.
nnermost chamber, a curtain wall.
nbound for Kadesh, the giants trail.
nbreed of the Father, a mansion is all.

Justice here prevails.
ubilee here never ends.
uryman here, the One who reigns.
ust folks here, no pretense!

Know the Lord your God.
neel before Him, His throne.
now-how of Ariel, this character.
nock all down at Jericho, the downer.

Lean not on your understanding.
earn dependent on Him.
east you should stumble.
eave all to the able.

Masterpiece of dust—now a foreigner.
anager of earth—now a stranger.
anna of the wilderness—now his failure.
an of the carnal—with no future.

No more shall he be of Marah.
ot or neither again of Taberah.
ow he is of Bethlehem.
oah's ark, where there is *lehem*.

On this mansion so divine.
pportune for the willing.
pen wide in a welcome.
ption is for certain.

Planted in the courts of His house.
lenteous fruit is thy course.
leasure and favor in His name.
lan of His infinite mind.

Questions asked are His proficiency.
uickened man by His Spirit holy.
uarters divided is the tree of the place.
uit not this honor, of this grace.

Rock of salvation is the Lord.
oute of righteousness accord.
oad to life is so narrow.
oyal piece of the morrow.

Still you be and trust Adonai.
tand you be, and see that day.
tore up riches of above.
teps of Him like a dove.

Thousand shall fall at thy feet.
he enemy shall flee before thee.
hen ten thousand at your side tumble.
hese seven ways, they shall hightail.

Utmost ether, His dwelling place.
nwearied souls, there laced.
nwavering plants, heaven's trees.
ncovering that hidden mass.

Vast fathoms, His splendor.
ain is far from His gander.
anity flees from His presence.
antage is the only case.

Worship now, you saints on high.
onderful His works undying.
ord of His breath, my life imprint.
orthy of His face, my light.

Yahweh reigns—forevermore.
our destiny's—sure avenue.
oke of freedom—purple ace.
ou are His *chosen race*.

Afterword

Have you wondered who exactly the person named Villa in my introduction of this book is? He is the very one who wrote this book. It is a name that I regard as a middle name, but I don't use it often anywhere, even at school or work. This book came about because of the earnest longing of my heart to know more about God. I was nobody in church, but no one knew my search for truth and what was going on in my heart. Only the Lord knew that. Out of the church, in my private times with the Lord, I asked so many questions that were terrible, silly, and funny, but most were good and meaningful concerning life. Yet I found that the Lord was and is always faithful to answer any questions asked by anyone anywhere because all that is around us, whether seen or unseen, were created and formed by Him. And the result of me asking so many questions is the book you are holding in your hand right now.

Since beginning writing in 2001, I didn't anticipate ever writing a book to publish. I was just writing poetry as a hobby until late 2013, when this urge to publish emerged in my heart in order to share what I had been writing and living for with others.

By the way, I am one of the believers who asks the Lord so many questions about everything that I read in the Bible. If the Lord were or is a human being, He would already be fed up with me and lob me out of His door or even His window, but nevertheless, He is always faithful, my God who is my *answer*. I believe that this kind of thought, of directly asking God, should be part of all Christians' lives, for it fulfills the promise of the new covenant that He gave us through His death on the cross.

Just to give an example, here are few of the questions that I have asked him since 2001:

Where and what were You doing when there was yet nothing? What or where is Your origin? Why did You create Satan? What did Abel actually offer symbolized by the "firstlings of his flock and the fat thereof," and so his brother who offered the vegetables? Why did Satan stand on the right hand of Joshua as they stood before You in heaven? Why did You change people's names that I read in the scriptures, and what does every one of those names mean? Why did You harden the heart of the Pharaoh of Egypt not to let Your people go when You Yourself had sent Moses to tell him to let them go? Why did you send the lying spirit to come down upon four hundred prophets who stood before King Ahab and his comrade? If Satan had won and got the body of Moses on Nebo, what would have been the story then? And why did You send the evil spirit to come upon King Saul while David played music with his hand before him? Which angel was actually the spirit of death whom You sent to kill every firstborn of Egypt? I want to know his or her name. What did the serpent look like before You got rid of its members from its body? Was the Tree of Knowledge a good or bad tree? And if it is good or bad, for what purpose did You place it there? Was the Tree of Knowledge a single tree or two separate trees? The rivers that parted and watered the garden of Eden are here, as we can see in this world. They are Pishon, Gihon, Tigris, and the Euphrates. But where is the garden now? Why did you create man on the sixth day and form him on the seventh day?

Seeing these examples, O beloved, how many questions have you asked the Lord in all your lifetime as a Christian about the Bible's contents or anything that is happening in this world today? And who do you ask often? Is it men or Christ the Spirit? I believe you must have gotten some answers to those. As for me, I have asked the Lord so much that I can't even remember, but I have kept the answers in my heart even until now. Thirteen years of questions is so much. And little of the many answers I got, you have read in this book in poetic format. Let it be, if God wills, I shall write another book soon.

My children sometimes ask their mum about the many books I keep in boxes in my room, which are in different sizes and types that I have bought at the local supermarket to write on since 2001.

Their mother would only say this, "He writes anything he can think of, see, overhear, or come across."

That is exactly the truth. And just recently, I told them that I would be submitting some of my notes for publishing. They marveled. They were very excited and very supportive.

There is one thing that I keep telling them and others whom I have the opportunity to share my heart with: anyone who believes in Jesus Christ is so privileged and fortunate because of who our God is. That is, "We can do all things through Christ who strengthens us." I am a mechanical tradesperson who works mainly in the factories, workshops, and machine shops—who deals mainly with spanners and tools—and it does not fit in to see a person like me writing a book about another field. Even writing itself is not the field I am in. It is just one of my favorite hobbies that I have enjoyed doing with my heart during my free time all these years.

The secret is the connection between the heart and mind. The heart is the center of your temple, the pulpit of the Lord, and the mind is the control tower of your world. If whatever one desires and longs for comes from the heart and connects it with the mind, it shall come to pass. That is what I believe in Christ.

And let me tell you this: it has been God's ongoing game to use the things that are foolish to confound the wise, and He uses the weaker things of this world to pull down the things that are mighty. The things that are poor and despised, He has regarded as His treasures and pleasures, thus displaying His wisdom. That is why He had chosen most of His disciples from the grassroots level.

How fortunate we are because of His promises to us. From the very core of my heart, I can say to you, beloved reader that God is beyond words. If only you shall seek Him with every beat and bit of your heart, you will come to know what I mean, and you will do so much more than what I have written for your instigation in this book. The seed I have sown to your heart today shall multiply and bear much and much more.

Some may say that they have known everything from Genesis to Revelation and don't need anything anymore. They have actually brought God down beneath their feet because they have narrowed and limited the capacity of God's endless, revealing power of His Word. Some say that knowing the deeper things of God belongs to the church frontiers and leaders only and not for commoners. They have turned down the promise of God pouring out His spirit upon all flesh, both great and small in this latter day. "For this is the covenant that I will make with the house of Israel after those days, saith the Lord; I will put my laws into their mind, and write them in their hearts: and I will be to them a God, and they shall be to me a people: And they shall not teach every man his neighbour, and every man his brother, saying, Know the Lord: for all shall know me, from the least to the greatest" (Heb. 8:10–11, KJV).

This is the new covenant: God himself firstly came down to reconcile and live with men after so long a time, doing away with the works of the law where a mediator (middleman) stands in between God and men. And by him doing so—having busted and broken the barriers, boundaries, and borders of isolation and separation that once began in the garden of Eden—hallelujah! Blessed be the Lord our God.

Once again, according to this new covenant, God wants each person to seek Him personally so He can commune with everyone that He may put His laws in our minds and write them in our hearts. And when that is done, no one will be able to teach the other person, even his brother, sister or neighbor about whom God really is and how He works, for every one of us shall know our God by heart.

Therefore, think about what you lack in life that is preventing you from advancing to knowing your God and Lord as never before. You have His Spirit! You have the Bible, and you are His temple! You are His predestined child to partake of His heavenly riches and treasures according to His promises, especially on this last day of the week. And so it is your heart—the pulpit of His holy temple that holds the key to your life—where His Word of truth shall proceed out and spring forth like a fountain, never to dry up again as He had promised to the Samaritan woman, which stands for the Gentile church.

I truly believe you have learned a lot by reading my book. My prayer is that you must never let this opportunity pass you by, and you shall discover for yourself the truth of who and how God is.

Can you imagine what the Lord will reveal to you more than what He had done to me? Remember—it is not an overnight gain. "Life in the Lord is to be lived." I beseech you, beloved, do what you ought to do, and you shall see His truth, Word, and promise to turn you into a miracle come true. May the grace of the Father of our Lord Jesus Christ be with you and bless you as never before while you live for Him, with Him, in Him, and by Him, now and forevermore.

Printed in the United States
By Bookmasters